66 Bible Sonnets

Other books by Blaine Turner:

Aoife's Bible

When Horses Fly

The King Is Coming

Beastmasters

The Dollhouse Trilogy

Trapped

Captive

Embraced

blaineturner.blogspot.com

66 Bible Sonnets

by

Blaine Turner

illustrated by

Anna Jamison

book title designs by

Titus Ulferts

foreword by

Jason DeRouchie

ISBN: 978-0-578-22426-8

All my Shakespearian sonnets consist of fourteen lines:
three quatrains (four-line stanzas) followed by a final couplet,
composed in iambic pentameter, with the rhyme scheme
ABAB CDCD EFEF GG.

Special thanks to Jean Turner for inspiration and augmentation.

Dedication

For my wife, Jean Crabtree Turner

A time but briefly tasted, fleeting sun,
A road now run and gone, a fleeing rail,
A ticket torn and tossed, the travel done—
Good memories, piles of stones to mark a trail.

The past aborts at our return, it seems,
A path found changed and cold for you and me.
Go back and time will alter all our dreams,
But dreaming back makes happy memory.

The people come and gone, the hands that shake,
The tears behind our eyes, the smiles we say,
The love we breathe, along the road a stake,
We drive another memory this way.

We've been too briefly two who walk as one,
To leave a lifetime of stakes and stones—LET'S RUN.

FOREWORD

Scripture's message put to verse,
Theology from Genesis to Revelation.
Skill with quill and lines that are terse;
God's glory in Christ given meditation.

Discipleship for the hungry heart;
Careful readings; a biblical summation.
Thoughtful and faithful from the start;
A journey from creation to consummation.

Moving from foundation unto fulfillment,
From shadow to substance and escalation,
Book by book, from Old to New Testament,
Anticipation to realization.

Christ would triumph through tribulation,
Overcoming curse through his righteous life.
Hope supplied unto every nation,
Divine wrath removed, salvation from strife.

The problem solved; the revealed mystery;
The splendor of the Son, the height of history.

———

Jason S. DeRouchie
Research Professor of Old Testament and Biblical Theology
Midwestern Baptist Theological Seminary

Impressions from
every book of the Bible

1 בְּרֵאשִׁית

Beginnings spoke by God is <u>Genesis</u>,
Created all and in His image, man;
But Adam sinned, then Cain, and lost their bliss;
And flood and rainbow spoke to Noah's clan.

From Babel scattered God chose Abraham;
In spite of Sodom's evil, God would bless;
Boy Isaac spared to bless son Jacob's scam,
Then Joseph sold to Egypt who oppress.

Yet what was meant for evil, God made good;
"I AM El-Shaddai, harken to My rod;
I covenant to you your nationhood
Placed on the land and I will be your God.

Though Satan bites the heel, his head will crush;
And Israel endures, God's blessings gush.

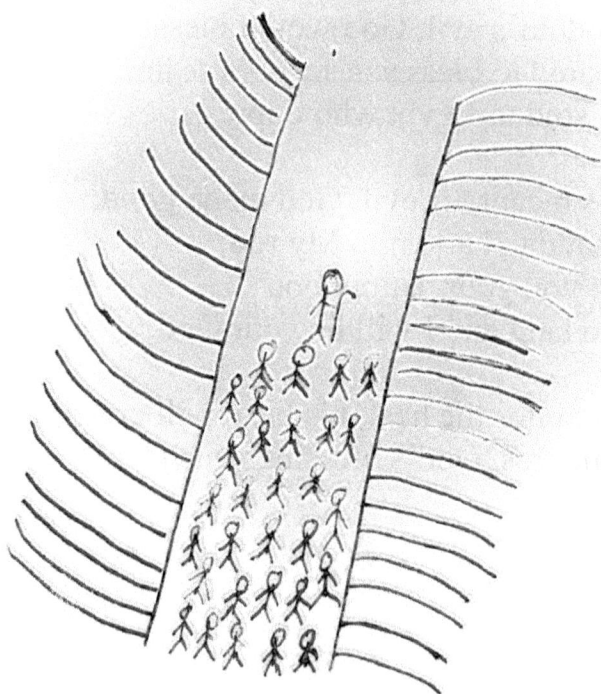

2 שְׁמוֹת

The <u>Exodus</u> to Sinai—sea divides
To lead the Israelites in covenant;
God spoke from in a fire bush confides,
"Go speak to Pharaoh." Moses said, "I can't."

The jealous God, in Egypt sent plagues ten,
And hardened pharaoh's heart—the firstborn die,
Except for Israel's passed over when
The blood on doorframes seen was Christ's. That's why.

The Ten Commandments carved on tablets stone,
But still they made a golden calf in sin;
So Moses pled that mercy please be shown;
He pitched God's tent but no one can go in.

I am I AM a jealous God of woe,
Who said to Pharaoh, "Let My people go."

Leviticus

scapegoat

High priest

3 וַיִּקְרָא

Leviticus: the LORD called FROM His tent:
Here's how to live with Me, a holy God;
Through sacred priests ordained you must repent,
By offerings of thanks, not just façade.

But Aaron's sons did mock God's holiness,
And died—which demonstrates that He is just;
Uncleanliness brings death; the pure He'll bless;
Integrity of moral life brings trust.

God's laws extend to every part of life,
To live apart from all the world around;
And yearly feasts atone for sin and strife;
The scapegoat shows that mercy will abound.

Obedience brings peace upon the land;
Unfaithfulness, disaster from God's hand.

Numbers

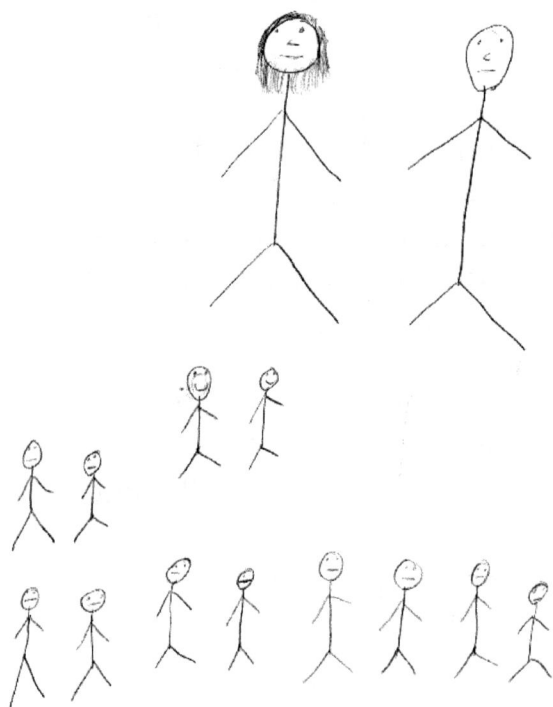

בְּמִדְבַּר 4

The LORD said <u>number</u> all of Israel;
He talked to Moses IN His holy tent;
And at their center, laws to keep them well—
"Return to Egypt!" they rebel, lament.

But twelve were sent to spy the land within;
"There're giants! We are doomed," said all but two;
Then Moses struck the water rock in sin,
So just the children ever would get through.

Rebellion-sin is judged by God with snakes,
So Moses prayed and raised a staff to heal;
And Balaam prophesied a star that takes
The splendid Heir of Jacob; all will kneel.

So may the LORD bless you and never cease,
His face to shine on you and give you peace.

Deuteronamy

דְּבָרִים 5

The "second law" is <u>Deuteronomy</u>
To Jews before they gain the Promised Land,
In faith to covenant that they would see
The blessings that can come from God's own hand.

So what does God demand but fear the LORD,
And walk obedient to Him and serve
In love with all the might you can afford;
He'll bless your hearts much more than you deserve.

This Moses asked them in his final breath:
God's curse or blessing—which do you hold dear?
Today I set before you life or death;
Shema is my most fervent call to hear:

Hear, Israel: the LORD our God is one;
Love Him with all you are, till life is done.

6 יְהוֹשֻׁעַ

The LORD told <u>Joshua</u> when Moses died,
Do keep this book of laws upon your lips,
And meditate by morn and eventide,
Obey, and sweetest milk and honey drips.

The Canaanite gal Rahab hides the spies,
Then Jericho's stout walls turn into sand,
But Achan steals God's spoils, so Ai cries,
Yet Jews in victory, divide the land.

If serving God seems evil unto you,
Then choose the gods—the ones our God abhorred;
But as for me and all my household too,
We know our God and we will serve the LORD.

Be strong and not discouraged, scared, or slow;
For God will be with you where'er you go.

שֹׁפְטִים 7

The LORD did cycle <u>Judges,</u> leaders all,
To rescue Israel from sin and shame,
To slay their foes in battle's bloody brawl;
Their love of Baal was certainly to blame.

So Ehud's left stabbed Eglon in the gut,
And Deborah's Jael tent pegged Sisera;
And God said, "Gideon, I'll save your butt;
Your fleece is proved in oozing viscera."

He made an ephod idol, worshipped gold,
And Samson's mighty hair Delilah chopped;
A Levite's concubine raped hundredfold,
Which led to civil war where thousands dropped.

Although I do what's right in my own eyes,
God keeps His promises and hears my cries.

רות 8

Poor <u>Ruth</u>'s a foreign widow, sweet of face;
Her bitter mom-in-law's dear husband died;
So she returns to Judah, her home place;
"Don't urge me leave you," loyal daughter cried.

"For where you go, there I will surely go,
and where you lodge, there I will always stay;
Your people will be always mine, I know,
Your God, my God, for now and every day."

In barley harvest, Boaz noticed her,
"Dear gleaning girl, I spread o'er you, my wings,
As kinsman, I redeem you, I concur."
So they were wed and saved the line of Kings.

And blessèd be the LORD who has this day
Redeemed a common person cast away.

1 Samuel

1 שְׁמוּאֵל 9

First Samuel starts as Hannah is ignored,
Though grief becomes all joyous at his birth;
For there is no one holy like the LORD;
There is no Rock quite like our God in worth.

The Jews all begged for kings like others had,
So Samuel thus anointed Saul to reign;
But he was proud, dishonest, sinned so bad,
And lost in battle, killed himself—insane.

But meanwhile God had called a shepherd boy,
Ten thousand foes like trophies on the shelf,
A man so after God's own heart for joy,
Who Jonathan loved, just as he loved himself.

This David slew Goliath with a stone;
His strength had come from God and God alone.

2 Samuel

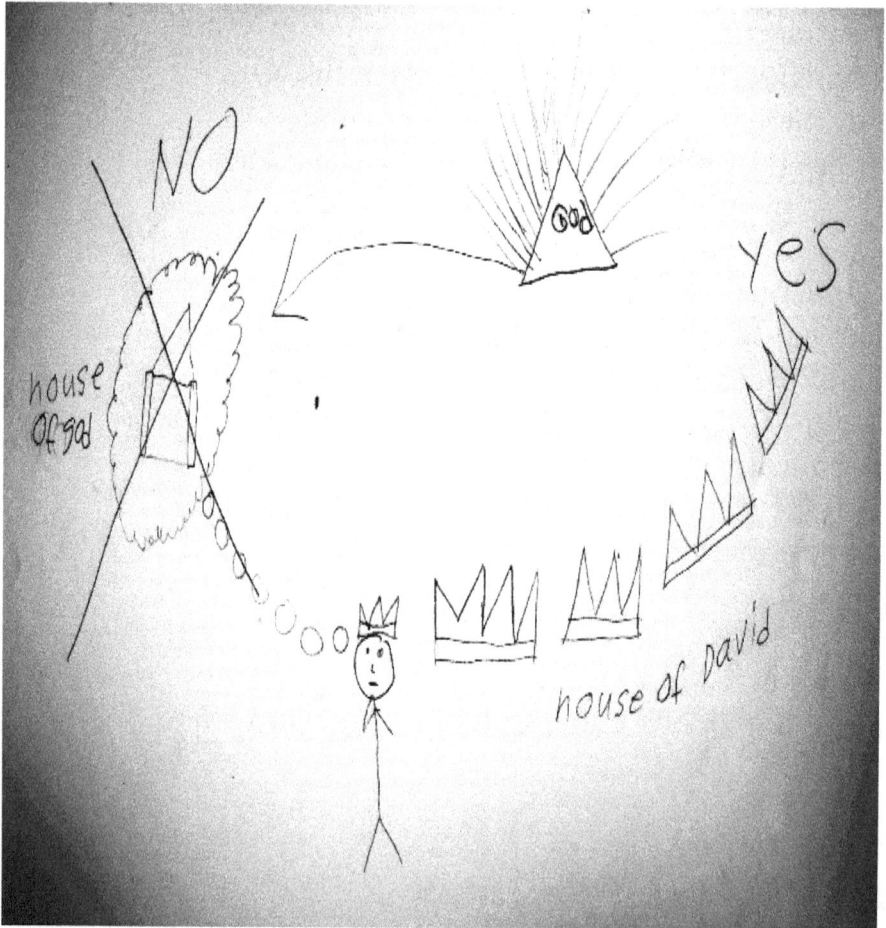

2 שְׁמוּאֵל 10

As <u>Samuel Two</u> continues, David reigns,
Laments King Saul, Jerusalem then takes;
A temple built by David, God distains;
Instead for David, lasting kingdom makes.

Then David's children messed up, unfulfilled;
First Amnon violated sis in bed,
So brother Absalom then had him killed,
And led rebellion as King David fled.

With mighty men, he fought the Philistines,
"My enemies all turned their backs and flew;
He girded me with strength, by every means;
The LORD's my fortress, my salvation true."

Who steals a poor man's lamb—a party throws?
You surely are that man—Bathsheba knows.

1 Kings

1 מְלָכִים 11

The <u>Kings,</u> <u>one</u> book, two parts with this the first
Where Solomon will sit on David's throne;
He asks for wisdom—life expertly versed,
And builds God's temple—their sins to atone.

But Solomon took wives and deities,
And slaves just like the Pharaoh king before;
So all the kingdom split, brought to its knees;
Some bad kings in the South, but North way more.

Elijah prophet spoke from God alone,
More powerful than Baal to bring down fire;
King Ahab, Jezebel He'll not condone,
Injustice and idolatry so dire.

As God's pure holy temple, how am I?
My kingdom split? My faith a blatant lie?

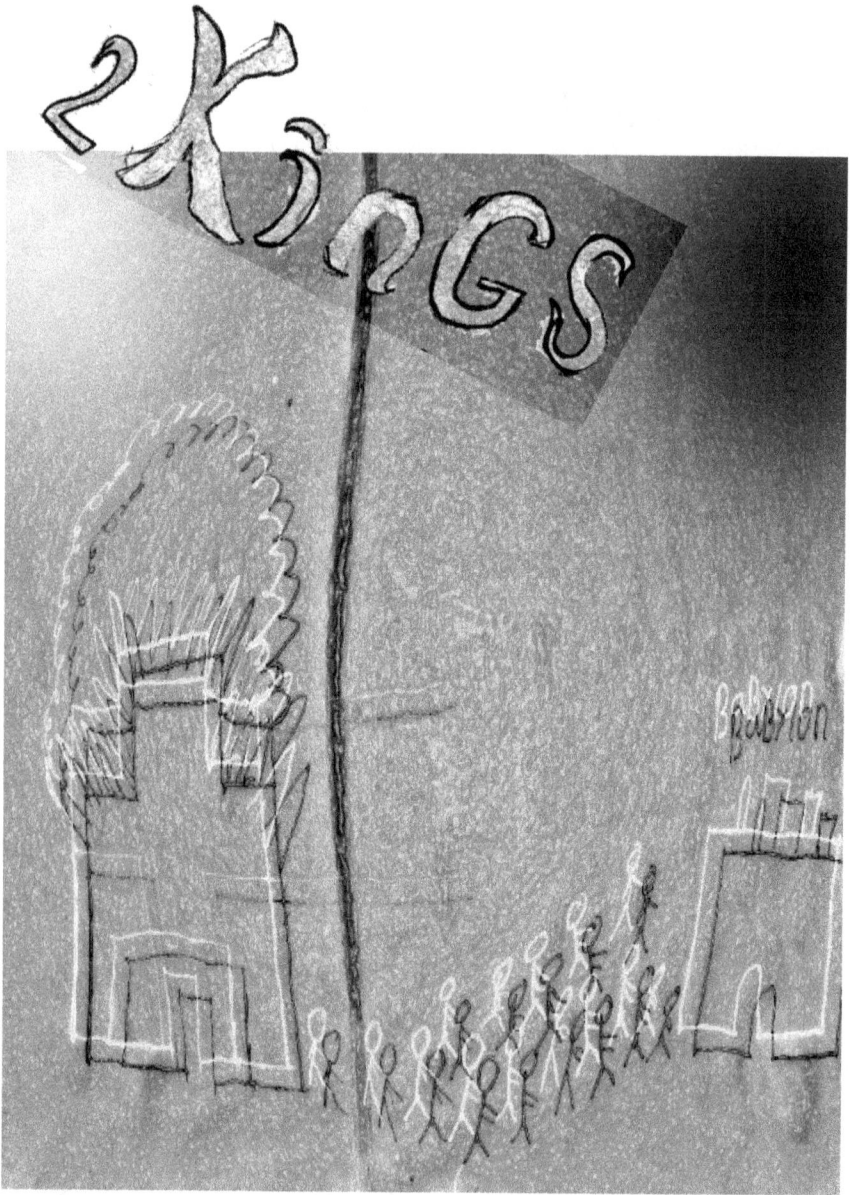

2 מְלָכִים 12

In <u>second</u> book of <u>Kings</u> Elisha grew,
Succeeds Elijah, miracles galore:
Heal leprosy, and purify the stew;
The axe head float, and dead to life restore.

The Northern Kingdom had some twenty kings,
And all were wicked, brought hysteria,
Idolatry, and other awful things,
Till they were exiled to Assyria.

The Southern Kingdom had Jerusalem,
And eight of twenty kings were mostly on,
But many prophets spoke of doom to them,
And Judah's dragged away to Babylon.

Is God almighty finished with the Jews?
Or even me, as Christ my heart renews?

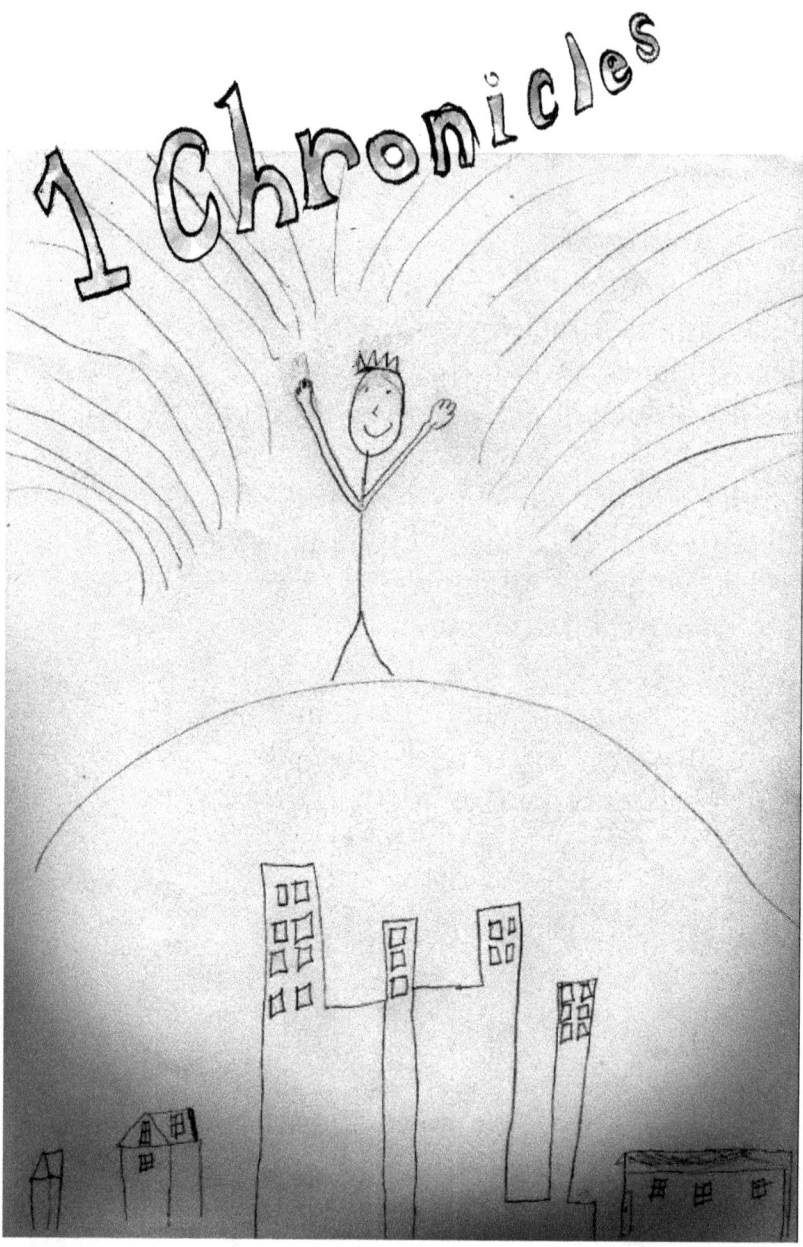

1 דִּבְרֵי הַיָּמִים 13

The <u>Chronicles</u> conclude the Hebrew book,
With tales about the past and future hope,
To image David as Messiah—look!
The genealogies—unbroken rope.

So David followed God and conquered all;
His fame spread quickly over every land,
The LORD made all the nations stand in awe,
So sing to God all peoples, how He's grand.

For God is great and greatly to be praised;
For all the other gods are without worth;
Ascribe to God all glory, stand amazed;
Now praise the LORD's salvation, all the earth!

Let heaven's gladness fill the hills and plains;
And say among the nations, "The LORD reigns!"

2 Chronicles

2 דִּבְרֵי הַיָּמִים 14

Two Chronicles begins with Solomon;
He prays to God as king that he be wise;
God also gave him riches by the ton;
He built God's temple—gold and great in size.

The kings obeying God were surely blessed;
"If people seek My face, and fold their hands,
And turn away from wicked ways confessed,
Then I forgive their sins and heal their lands."

Unfaithful kings brought pain, calamity,
Since they forsook the LORD—put Him at odds;
Jehoshaphat though, prayed his God to see;
Fear not, the battle is not yours, but God's.

Says Cyrus, "Those of you that God does know,
The LORD their God be with them—let them go."

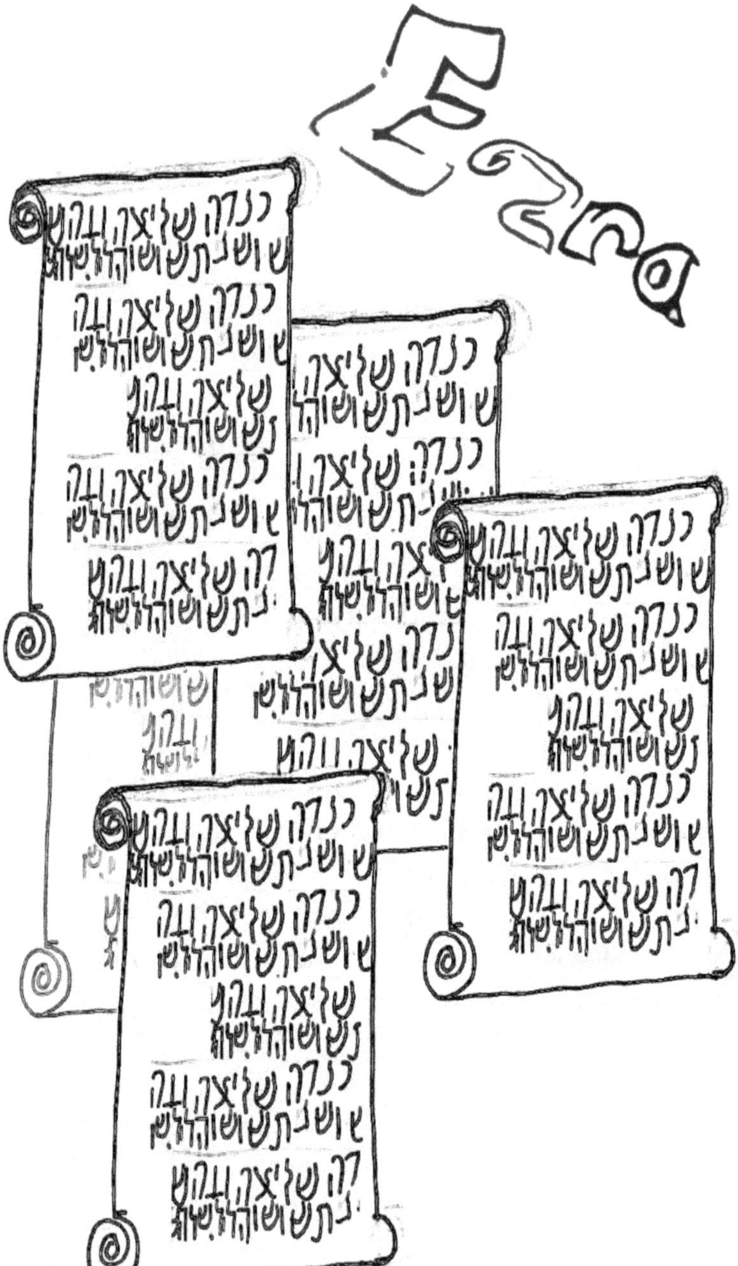
Ezra

15   עֶזְרָא

As <u>Ezra</u> starts, Zerubbabel returns,
To build Jerusalem's flat temple new;
King Cyrus sent him as God's call he learns,
And many came with gold cups—not a few.

Some folks not exiled wanted to help build,
Were told that they had not a part in it;
When finished, elders eyes with tears were filled,
"It's smaller than the old one—so unfit."

Then Ezra came to teach the Torah scrolls,
"Divorce your foreign wives, throw out by force;
And set apart yourselves to have pure souls,
Avoid the pagan girls—God hates divorce."

The leaders fail, although we know they're smart;
The people really need a brand new heart.

Nehemiah

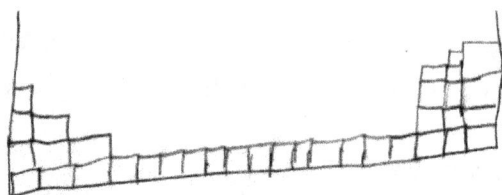

16   נְחֶמְיָה

Let <u>Nehemiah</u> go—his dream fulfilled—
Repair the walls around Jerusalem;
Once there, he said, "Come guys, let us rebuild,
Not Arabs though—we'll not be joined with them."

So then comes spiritual renewal—feast:
Confessing sin, affirming covenant,
And vows to follow Torah, never ceased;
The feast of Booths—all Israel did chant.

Then Sabbath was dishonored, work was done,
The Temple was neglected, priests not fed,
And Jews did marry foreign girls for fun;
"I forced on them respect for God instead.

"Remember me, oh gracious God, for good,
At least I tried to cleanse them—best I could."

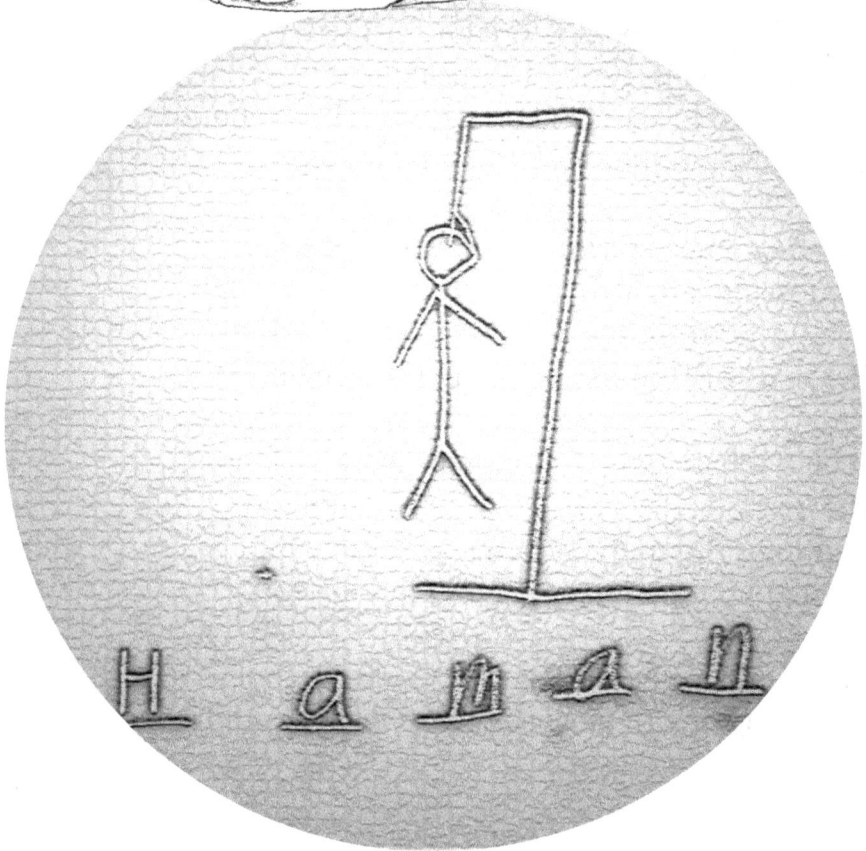

אֶסְתֵּר 17

The lovely <u>Esther</u> pleased the Persian King,
Who'd sacked his queen—dance lewd, she'd not agreed;
As parties raged, all bowed to Haman's ring,
Save Mordecai, whose death it was decreed.

Thus Haman built a gallows for all Jews,
But Mordechai had shown the king a plot,
So he made Haman honor, not accuse—
A guy was hanged but not quite whom he thought.

Since Esther dared approach the King unbid,
Inviting them to banquets to request
That Haman's plan to kill would be undid—
He met his death instead; you know the rest.

The Jews fought back at Purim, saved the day,
As God protects His own in every way.

18 אִיּוֹב

The LORD said, "Satan, you may test My <u>Job</u>,
A blameless servant you can mortify;"
His family lost, and ashes for a robe,
Pus boils scraped, despair! Curse God and die.

"I'm innocent, my suffering's not just."
"But God is just; you must have sinned, or will."
"The LORD has given, all returns to dust."
"You've my defense, so God, why now so still?"

"Does Job give horses might or flight to birds?"
"Oh God, I now repent my thoughts too bold,
And in my flesh I know and love Your words."
And so the LORD restored to Job two fold.

No purpose thwarted, God condemns, forgives,
And now I know that my Redeemer lives.

Psalms

PSALM 139:23

תְּהִלִּים 19

In <u>Psalms</u> man's poems sing lament and praise,
To God my LORD, Messiah, reigning King;
My lamp, my shepherd, steadfast all my days,
I know I shall not want for anything.

My God, my God, have You forsaken me?
"Be still and know that I am here," You say;
If weeping lasts all night, then joy bursts free,
Rejoice! It comes by grace with each new day.

Your hidden Word in me says God is there,
And He who came in His dear blessèd name,
Became my rock, my Savior, my sweet prayer;
His steadfast love endures; that's why He came.

The LORD, the God of Israel be blessed,
And in my heart "Amen" in love expressed.

20 מִשְׁלֵי

From <u>Proverbs</u> spring advice, spill wisdom rich,
Upon us children bound as folly's fools,
Not spared the rod, thus saved from sin's dark ditch,
By parents' guiding hands and gentle rules.

Above all else you do, please guard your hearts,
For all life issues, guarded hearts entail;
So trust the LORD, and not your own fake smarts;
Our God has plans; His purposes prevail.

As iron sharpens iron, here we stand,
In knowledge precious, more than gems or gold;
Our faces wrinkle, yet the tongue stays grand;
No, only Wisdom can abide and hold.

In all our ways acknowledge God our LORD,
A tower strong and safe from every sword.

ECCLESIASTES

21 קֹהֶלֶת

Ecclesiastes: everything is mist,
So hevel, hevel—smoke is here, then done;
The wind blows round and round, and that's the jist;
There's nothing new here under God's bright sun.

O there's a time for everything of worth—
A time to weep, to laugh, and dance a lot—
A time for war, a time for peace on earth;
But men of old will die and be forgot.

Yes, fools will fold their hands till ruin starts,
But God has made all beautiful in time,
And also set eternity in hearts;
Yet who can fathom our dear God in rhyme?

Fear God's command; this is your duty, man—
All secrets judged in God's eternal plan.

Song of songs

שִׁיר הַשִּׁירִים 22

כלה שלי אהובה שיר השירים אהוב,   My darling bride, beloved Song of Songs,

שושנת שושן הליל של העמק,   A rose of Sharon, Lily of the vale,

בואי איתי ותחושי את הקסם של פריחת אהבתנו,   Do come with me, see where love's bloom belongs;

יונתי תזדקפי – לעולם לא ניכשל ולא נתעייף   Arise my dove—we shall not faint or fail.

הצבי היפה תואר וגם האיילה מהלכים להם על ההרים   My handsome stag, gazelle on mountains fine,

חזור אלי כי ליבי תפור עם ליבך,   Come back to me; my heart so pants for you;

תסתכל אלי כי אהבתי בשבילך ואהבתך היא בשבילי,   Oh look! My love is his and he is mine;

דגל הנאמנות מונף בגאווה מעל לראש שלי.   His banner over me is faithful true.

אוצר המלך אינו יכול לקנות את שדיה המעוררים,   Her breasts aroused, no king can ever buy;

נשיקתה היא עונג כה עמוק ממש כאן ליד דלתי,   Her kiss such deep delight, here at my door;

הגן שלנו נהיה רענן ולח ביחד עם כל אנחה,   Our garden fresh and wet with every sigh,

הלהט שלי אלייך ילך ויתחזק לנצח.   Will last, my fawn, and grow forever more.

אהבתנו חזקה כמוות והיא חתומה לנצח,   Our love is strong as death—sweet-sealed to stay,

גם מים רבים לא יוכלו לשטוף את אהבתנו עימם.   That many waters cannot wash away.

Isaiah

23 יְשַׁעְיָהוּ

Isaiah writes the words of God, behold,
A virgin bears a son, Emmanuel—
Our God with us, so comfort ye, enfold—
A child is born to us, the angels tell.

Called Wonderful, the government is sealed,
Called Counsellor, Strong God, the Prince of Peace,
The Everlasting Father, now revealed,
So bring glad tidings, lights that never cease.

For You were pierced for our transgressions through,
Unjustly crushed—it's us who are depraved—
And our just punishment was put on You,
Despised, rejected—by Your wounds we're saved.

For we, like sheep have surely gone astray,
And each of us has gone to his own way.

Jeremiah

7 The word that came to Jeremiah from the Lord, saying, "Stand in the gate of the Lord's house and proclaim there this word and say, 'Hear the word of the Lord, all you of Judah, who enter by these gates to worship the Lord!'"Thus says the Lord of hosts, the God of Israel, "Amend your ways and your deeds, and I will let you dwell in this place.

24 יִרְמְיָהוּ

Before I formed you <u>Jeremiah</u> born,
I knew you in the womb, set you apart,
Appointed to the nations to forewarn
Of pending judgement and a brand-new heart.

Bad Babylon will come destroy the Jews,
Jerusalem exiled years seventy,
Until the LORD, the nation sure renews,
In sweet New Covenant security.

How bless'd to trust the LORD in confidence,
To seek and find with all your heart's delight;
You're not too young to eat my words and hence
To say whatever God commands as right.

God knows the plans He has to prosper you;
No harm will come—bright future will ensue.

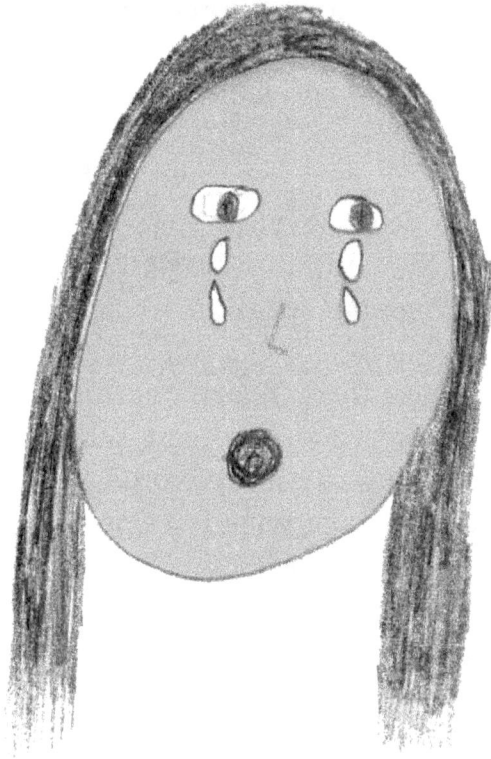

Lamentations

25 אֵיכָה

I weep in <u>Lamentations</u> for my love;
My country plays the whore—she lost my trust;
She worships sun and moon, but kills the dove;
Beneath her skirts its blood pain cries of lust.

She weeps but all her loves abandon her;
Her children run away, all captive now;
For greed and pride become the saboteur,
They spit on God, and laugh, and break their vow.

Will not the sovereign LORD soon bend His bow,
To pierce and swallow up our palaces?
And He who gave this land becomes our foe;
While leaders sit and lick their calluses.

But great in faithfulness, the God we knew;
His mercies every morning will renew.

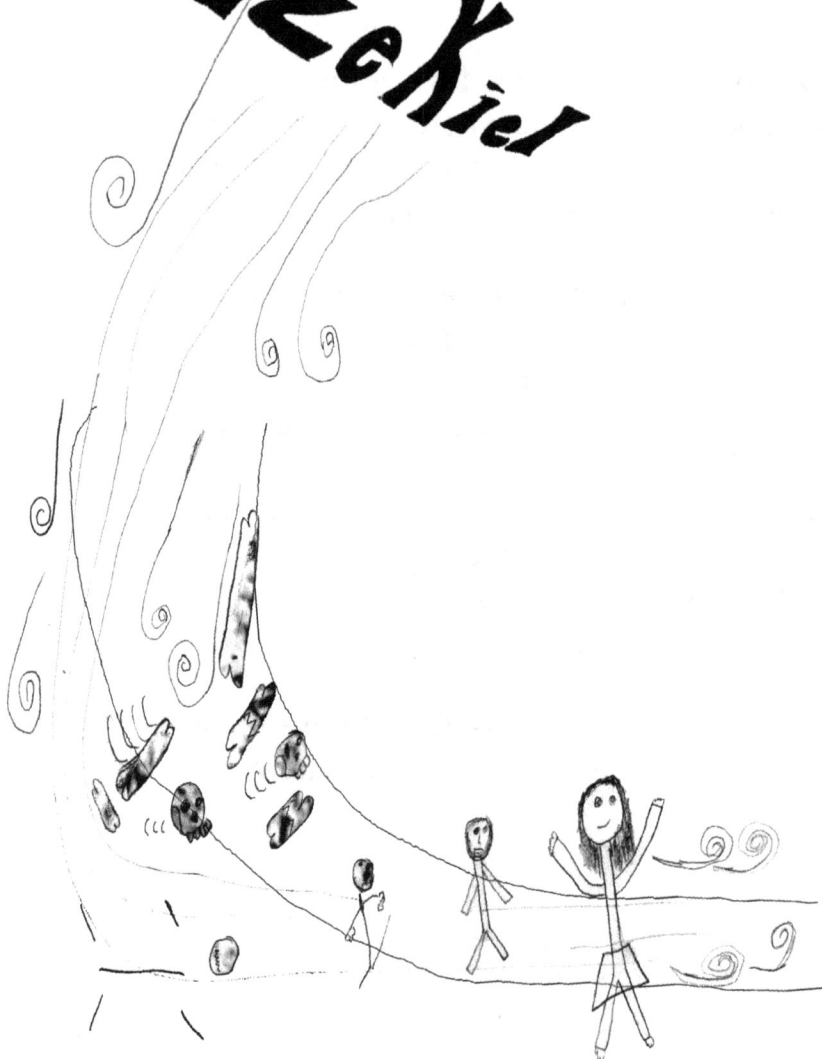

26 יְחֶזְקֵאל

Ezekiel's God connected dry bones found,
From toe bone, foot bone, shin bone—all dem bone,
The hip bone, back bone, head bone, walk around,
There in the valley, hear God's word alone.

The Spirit gave them flesh, breathed life that day,
To show there's hope for all—though judgement looms,
For our idolatry drives God away;
Still He defeats all evil, any dooms.

God's glory's manifested as a dream:
At fire's center four live creatures flew,
On wings like lightning—wheels and eyes all seem
Like God's clear presence in His kingdom new.

My God will take my broken heart of stone—
Replace it with a heart of flesh alone.

27 דָּנִיֵּאל

The prophet <u>Daniel</u> exiled, serves the king,
With Shadrach, Meshach, and Abednego,
Who Babylon's high praise refused to sing;
So God delivered them from fires aglow.

Then Daniel wouldn't eat the king's rich foods,
He prayed to God, so surely that meant death,
He's cast in den of lions in bad moods,
But God did close their mouths, we hold our breath.

In Daniel's dreams, God sends a Son of Man,
To be exalted over empire kings,
Who end up eating grass; it's all they can,
Repent or be destroyed, that's what God brings.

Most human beings **will** turn into beasts,
But God has promised **I** won't be the feast.

28 וְשֵׁעַ

Hosea, go and wed a whore of lust;
Raise children bred in her unfaithfulness;
But I can't have a nest of broken trust—
For I am love—defiled I'll never bless.

Your son will pay for bloodshed in the land;
Your daughter named Unloved, My mercy's done;
Your next born boy not even in My hand—
By idols raped and allies overrun.

So understand My paths are true and right,
And walk in them My sweet and sorry bride;
And when you fall, your LORD will hold you tight,
And keep you safe, redeemed, and by My side.

Who sows the wind will reap the mad wind's whirl;
Yet I will love and heal My wayward girl.

29 יוֹאֵל

Past sin, says <u>Joel</u>, becomes God's mercy hope,
A locust swarm, a sure repentance call;
The crops are dead—despair—the end of rope;
LORD, spare Your people, lest they perish all.

So God was filled with passion for His own,
Defeated all invaders, healed the land,
Indwelled the temple, mercy was well shown—
Disaster led to hope, as God had planned.

But nations, judgement in the valley wait;
The sun grows dark, the LORD's great voice will roar;
Yet, He's a fort for His to congregate;
He'll dwell with them and on them pardon pour.

Return to Me with your pure love that flows,
And rend your hearts and not your garment clothes.

30 עָמוֹס

To prophet <u>Amos</u>, Yahweh speaks to say
That justice rolls as rivers like a sword;
And does a lion roar without his prey?
All nations hung on meat hooks, says the LORD.

The LORD of hosts, who makes the mountains melt,
Who takes the sea and pours it on the land,
Despises your religion not heartfelt,
Sends fire all your walls cannot withstand.

Yet God will raise up David's fallen booth,
Rebuild it as it was when days were fine;
He'll plant it on their land, forever truth,
And mountains drip the sweet and flowing wine.

A plumb line God has set for Israel;
When will He spare them? When will all be well?

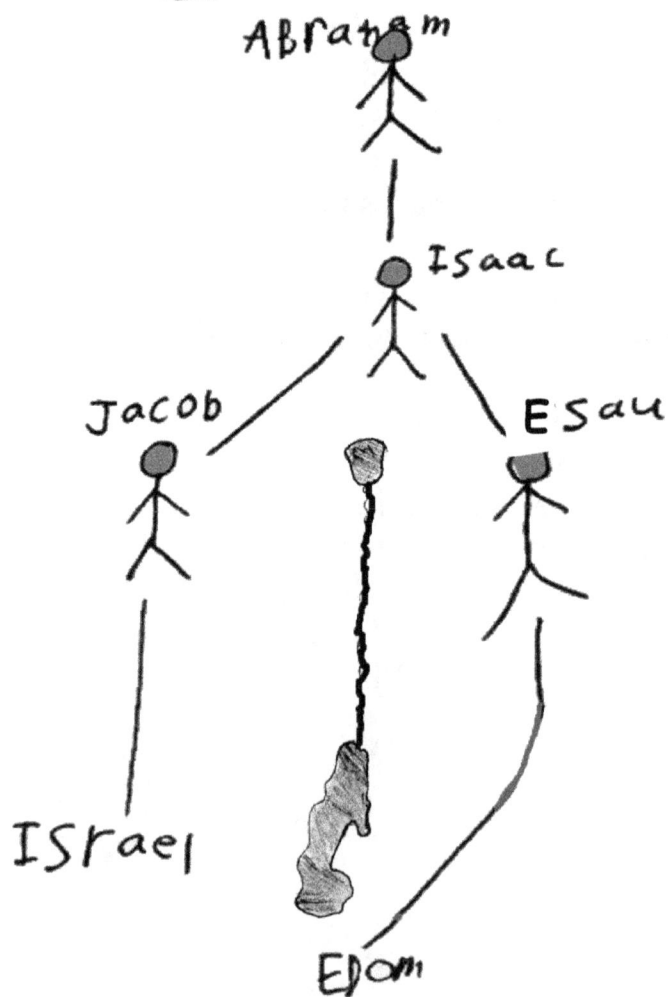

31 עֹבַדְיָה

The LORD gave <u>Obadiah</u> prophesy
Against the seed of Esau—Edomites
Trashed Israel in their calamity,
As Babylon sacked them in bloody fights.

The LORD said, "Edom, you're cut down to size,
Since you should not have plundered relatives,
And so, as you have done to Mine, likewise
You'll swallow punishment My wrath soon gives."

Jerusalem, though, will become safe land;
God's people will return, His praise to sing,
And capture Edom, God's domains expand;
All nations joined as one—the LORD is king.

So Edom's pride's disturbingly like mine—
Rejoice! In God's new kingdom I'll be fine.

Jonah

32 יוֹנָה

Poor <u>Jonah</u> sailed the other way when told
To preach to Nineveh, the enemy;
But God's compassion true and grace of old,
Sent storm and fish, three days to hear his plea.

He prophesied, "Your place be overturned!"
So king and people, even beasts repent.
"Just let me die," the prophet's fury burned;
He's mad that God would hear their sad lament.

So Jonah on a sunny hill did wait,
God sent a worm to eat his shady vine,
"Oh, Jonah, you feel anger at their fate;
But prophet, are your cares more yours or Mine?"

Alas, when God so blesses those I hate,
What then do I, in haste, articulate?

33 מִיכָה

God's <u>Micah</u> shows us what is good for me,
And what the LORD requires from those He loves:
Act justly, love God's mercy, humble be;
Oh, will the LORD be pleased with blood from doves?

The LORD confronts when evil greed begins;
Injustice rampant leads to coming woe;
But who's a God like You to pardon sins?
His remnant, all forgiven, heaven go.

So God will judge the peoples; they will beat
Their swords to plowshares—spears to pruning hooks;
The nations stand and fall at their gods' feet,
But we will walk with God as told in Books.

You Bethlehem Ephrathah are so small,
But out of you will come the King of all.

nahum

34 נַחוּם

Says <u>Nahum</u>: God brings vengeance on His foes,
But slow to anger, yet He breaks the rocks;
The LORD is good, a refuge in our woes,
Protects the sheep who run inside His flock.

Assyria is like a pool now dried,
As she is pillaged, plundered, ruined, ripped
By Babylon, the sword by which she died;
Her chariots are burned, her treasure stripped.

So woe to Nineveh, consumed in flame;
Oh king, your shepherds sleep, sheep run away,
The God against you lifts your skirts to shame,
And shows the nations nakedness that day.

Assyria's rise and fall just goes to show
How God will not let evil empires grow.

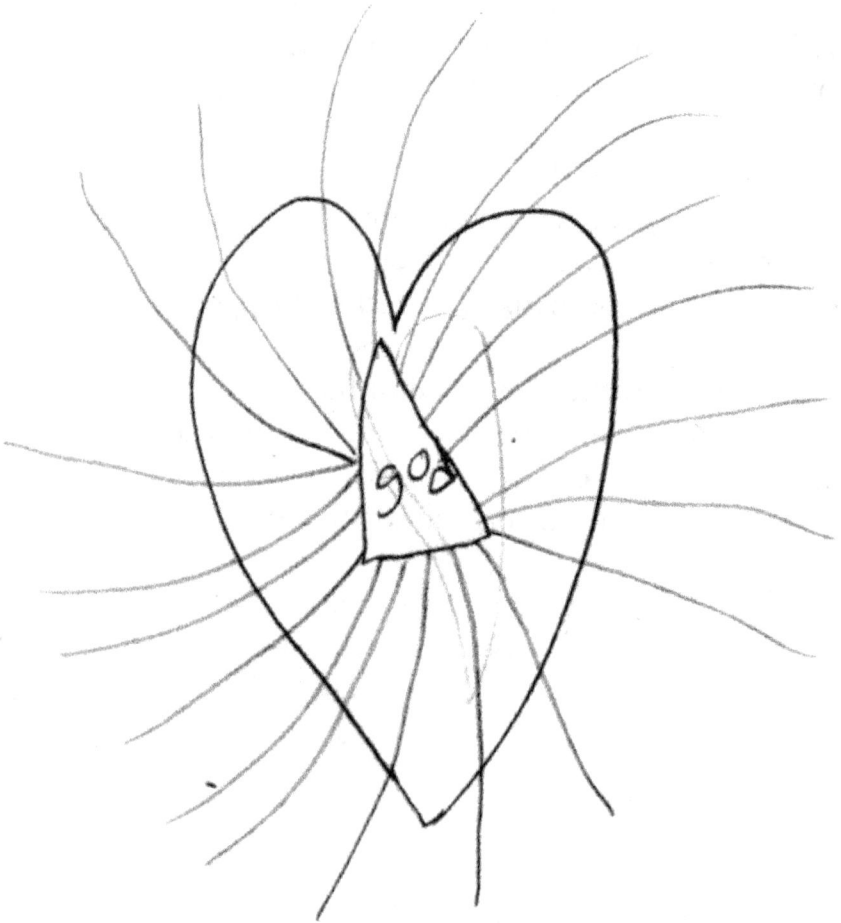

HabaKKuK

35 חֲבַקּוּק

The prophesy <u>Habakkuk</u> did receive:
When he complains that God is mute, won't hear
That Judah is corrupt and won't believe;
And Torah trashed in violence and fear.

But God says, "Prophet, you've seen nothing yet;
I'm sending Babylon; you're dragged away;
The woes they bring are worse; you'll be upset;
Yet I will bring them down in shame someday."

I shake, but wait—disaster soon will strike,
And fig trees lose their blossoms—boy oh boy;
All crops are dead, the grapes and flocks alike—
Yet I rejoice in God, my steadfast joy.

The sovereign LORD, my Savior, makes me strong,
Surefooted as the deer hooves all day long.

36 צְפַנְיָה

From <u>Zephaniah</u>, harken lest you fall;
Jerusalem be judged, day of the LORD.
You priests of Judah now profane the Law;
You people, so complacent, feel the sword.

Thus all the nations fall by Babylon:
The great Assyrians and Philistines,
With Moabites and Amorites are gone;
And God's own people face destruction scenes.

But not to death—to purify instead,
Unite all nations into family,
To call upon the LORD in humble dread;
And He will live among them faithfully.

The mighty Warrior Savior, just and strong,
Rejoices over even me in song.

חַגַּי 37

The LORD called <u>Haggai</u>: Tell all Israel,
"You build your house—My temple why delay?
You live in luxury—where shall I dwell?
Rebellion makes My blessings go away."

I'm ritually impure—I touched the dead;
Will food I touch become defiled as well?
The priests said "Yes." "But you," the LORD then said,
"Your offerings are tainted—your sins smell."

The LORD called Haggai: Tell Zerubbabel,
That I will shake the heavens and the earth,
And I will honor you, My signet full;
The LORD of hosts will bless and bring great worth.

So, do you lust for gold God blows away?
No! Build His temple—make Him king today.

38 זְכַרְיָה

Dreams <u>Zechariah</u>: Jews turn back to God,
And don't be like your ancestors in sins;
You talk repent but then act very odd;
Four horsemen ride patrol as peace begins.

The seventy long years of exile wanes;
The time for messianic kingdom nears;
O Israel recall past sin and chains,
Assyria, Babylon, and Persia fears.

Jerusalem is measured by the scroll,
A beacon to the nations, purified—
Called to be faithful, Prince Zerubbabel—
Yet coming Shepherd will be scorned and tried.

Rejoice, your King is like a thunderbolt,
But humble, righteous—riding donkey colt.

Malachi

39 מַלְאָכִי

God's <u>Malachi</u> shows Israel corrupts;
They doubt the love of God is paradise;
God's house is trashed, idolatry erupts;
He smears their face with dung from sacrifice.

"My name be honored, else be cursed you now,
Like marriage vows, be loyal just to Me;
I hate divorce; do not profane our vow;
The nations praise Me, all for you to see."

At Day of Judgement, wicked burn like straw,
But you'll be free like calves that leap for fun,
When led to pastures green; LORD blesses all,
But silence—till comes news of God's own Son.

Remember Moses' Torah—I will send
Elijah 'fore that Day, your hearts to mend.

40 Ματθαῖον

New Moses, Christ Messiah, <u>Matthew</u> stressed,
A gentle heart seeks ours, Emanuel;
So come to Him and He will give you rest
According to your faith, in Kingdom dwell.

The sparrows neither sow, nor reap, nor dress,
But God tends them; aren't you of greater worth?
And blessed are those who hunger righteousness,
For they'll be satisfied, bright lights on earth.

Judge not, for by that measure you'll be tried;
Be always humble children in His sight;
Though innocent, the Lamb was crucified;
Was killed but rose again for our own plight.

So let your salt spread all throughout the world—
I pray His word remains in me unfurled.

MARK

And what do you benefit if you gain the whole world but lose your own Soul

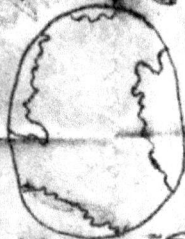

Mark 8:36

41 Μᾶρκον

Mark's Gospel speaks of Christ, the Son of Man,
And John baptized the Lord, His prep for toil;
His kingdom came, and save the lame, He can;
O mustard seed of faith, have you good soil?

So who is this? The victor king of Jews,
Or suff'ring servant, sword be stayed by love?
To die for us, can death become Good News?
Transfigured glow, beloved Son above.

Jerusalem! He enters riding tall;
Hosanna! Jesus Christ the tables turns;
The Lamb would die, the temple city fall,
But Christ would rise again as Satan burns.

Was He the Son of God in everything?
Could crucified Christ Jesus be my king?

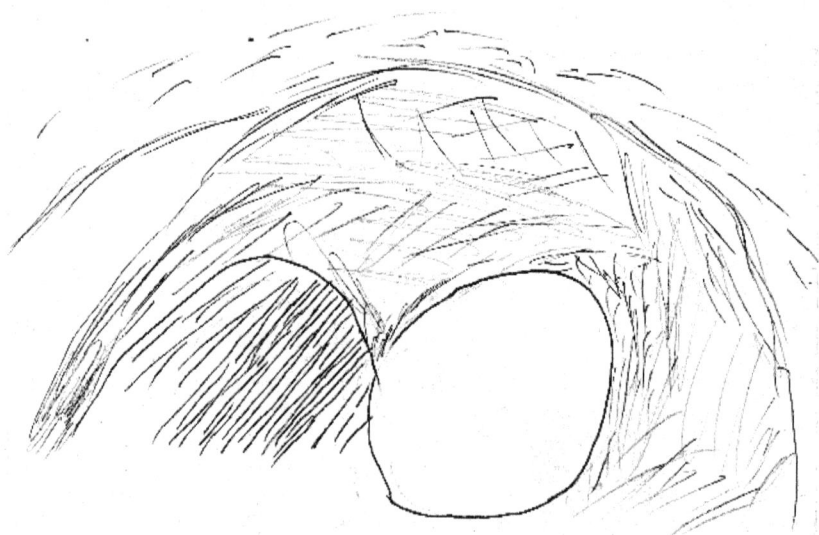

42 Λουκᾶν

Physician <u>Luke</u> portrays the Gospel heart,
That Christ was born and died and rose again;
Through parables His teaching to impart,
Fulfilling Scripture, He should suffer then.

So in the garden, prays His cup may pass,
"But not My will," says Christ, "but Thine alone."
Betrayed and tried, then scourged, He took their sass;
Though silent when accused, His face still shone.

Then nailed in pain to wood, for our own sin,
And naked, breathed His last to finish it;
Ripped from His Father's heart, the lost to win;
Our Father, to Thy name I shall commit.

And why still seek for life among the dead?
A risen Christ indeed now lives instead*!*

43 Ἰωάννην

The Word with God—writes <u>John</u>—was wholly God;
As Christ, I AM the life, the truth, the way,
The Word made flesh, a sorry trail to trod,
That dead in sin be born anew this day.

"So you are branches, I am your true vine;
As Lamb of God, I'll take away your sin;
As Shepherd, you My sheep will know you're Mine;
As Light and Love, I'll always hold you in.

So now you hear the truth that sets you free;
From water, wine—My wonders never cease;
Unless you're born again, you don't know Me;
I am the resurrection—hope and peace."

For God so loved the world, He sent His Son;
Believers now are saved, yes every one.

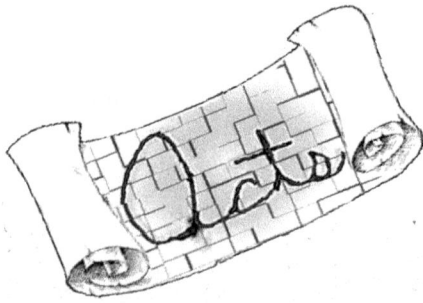

44 Πράξεις Ἀποστόλων

Luke scribes the <u>Acts</u> Christ's followers desire;
The resurrected Lord eats fish, and then
At Pentecost imparts God's wind and fire,
That they obey His Word, not follow men.

Said Peter, "Gold and silver have I none,
But what I have, I give—rise up and walk."
Repent, receive the Spirit and the Son;
As Christians, don't resist stoned Stephen's talk.

Then Saul became Apostle Paul to see
The gentiles grafted to the Church on earth;
He's tried for resurrection's hope to be,
In prison pens epistles of great worth.

I'm saved through grace but life has value lost,
If I am not his voice at any cost.

45 Ῥωμαίους

"For I am not ashamed," writes Paul to <u>Rome</u>;
The Gospel is our God's salvation pow'r;
For all have sinned, yet Christ redeems us home
Through faith, not law, and God's free blessing show'r.

While dead as sinners, Christ did die for us;
His gift is then eternal life above;
He works all things for good; He loves us thus,
And nothing separates us from this love.

Our God is faithful to His Israel—
Confess that risen Jesus Christ is Lord,
And you'll be saved through faith by hearing well
The Word of Christ, the sharp and two-edged sword.

O church, unite, hold fast to love, forgive,
Discern God's will—the joyous way to live.

1 Corinthians

Love

LOVE

46 Κορινθίους α'

Apostle Paul to <u>Corinth</u> tempest tossed,
Brings godly unity of thought and mind;
The cross is foolishness seen by the lost,
But to the saved is Pow'r of God assigned.

So flee from every immorality,
For that is not a holy kingdom right.
Your bodies, temples flaunt carnality?
No! Sanctify in Holy Spirit's might.

Christ's resurrection victory avowed,
Means love is kind and we will never die;
His love so patient, true and never proud,
Will transform us by faith in blink of eye.

I was a foolish kid of push and shove;
Now as a man I know the way of love.

47 Κορινθίους β′

In <u>Two Corinthians</u> Paul writes to say
That those in Christ are new creations now;
We have this treasure shown in jars of clay,
Afflicted but not crushed—God's power's vow.

Whoever sows just sparingly reaps same,
So give all cheerfully and God supplies;
I have my thorn but grace sufficient came;
Do not be yoked to unbeliever lies.

The super loud and flash "apostles" vent,
For they are false, deceitful workers—fake,
And we demolish all their argument,
Conform to Christ our Lord—we undertake.

We fix our eyes on things unseen but right;
We live by faith in God and not by sight.

Galatians

48 Γαλάτας

Galatians, there is neither slave nor free,
Not Jew or Gentile, male or female—Why?
For you're all one in Jesus Christ, you see,
He grants us freedom—we will never die.

We're never justified by works of law,
But steadfast faith in Jesus Christ alone;
We sowed, so thus a harvest time we saw,
For God cannot be mocked—so clearly shown.

The Spirit's fruit is joy, love, patience, peace.
I am astonished you so quickly run
To different gospels you have let increase,
Can't save—aside from Jesus there is none.

I'm crucified with Christ—no longer live,
Except by faith in Him—my life to give.

49 Ἐφεσίους

Ephesians, love predestined us as sons,
Adopted by His will, and not our works,
When we, quite dead in sin, yet His dear ones,
Were saved by purpose, never lucky quirks.

We're made alive; we're new, filled up with Christ,
Such rich diversity, one Spirit host;
Through resurrection pow'r, once sacrificed,
We gained His vict'ry peace; In God we boast!

So therefore, singing praise and thanks to all,
In union put off anger, lies and lust;
And run your house in love; your Christ recall;
And fear not fiery darts; His armor trust.

For grace, through faith, ends my salvation search;
Christ made us one, with gifts to build His church.

50 Πιλιππησίους

In chains Paul writes <u>Philippians</u> in love,
In trust that who began work not in vain,
Completes it on the Day of Christ above;
Paul knows to live is Christ—to die is gain.

Christ won't exploit equality with God;
Was born a servant man, in death to bless;
And now receives the highest holy nod,
So every knee should bow and tongue confess.

And all my fleshly works—a pile of crap,
Compared to faith in Christ, my righteousness,
A citizen of heav'n with Christ my map,
Content with Christ, my strength, as on I press.

Be never anxious, God is near—but pray;
Whatever's true, whatever's pure—think YAY!

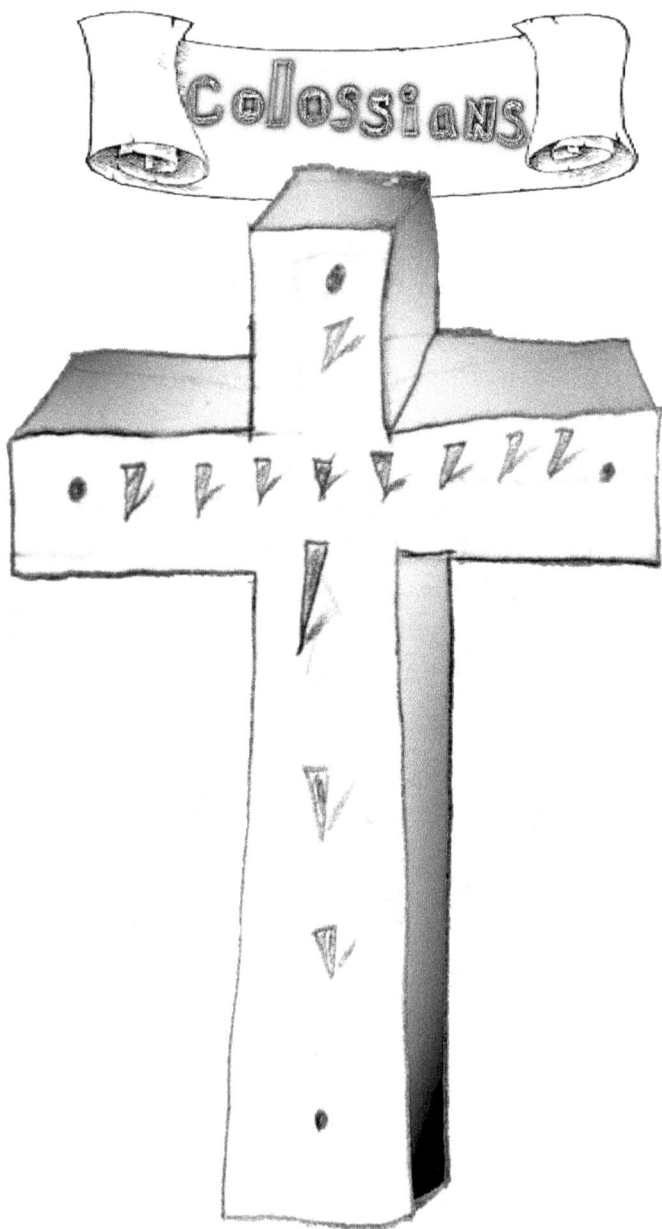

Colossians

51 Κολοσσαεῖς

Colossians, God's loved chosen people dear,
Do clothe yourselves with kindness, gentleness,
And let Christ's message dwell within you clear,
Admonish one another—wisdom bless.

Be sure that no one makes you sick or fall,
Through hollow and corrupt philosophy;
God's fullness dwells as Christ created all,
And heads the Church, His body, where we be.

You wives submit; you husbands love your brides;
You kids obey your parents every day;
You fathers don't provoke your kids, but guide;
Work hard as for the Lord in every way.

Since you are raised with Christ there is no loss;
For all your sins are nailed right to the cross.

1 Thessalonians

52 Θεσσαλονικεις α´

First Thessalonians, writes Paul to bless,
Their suffering identified with Christ;
May God increase hope, love, and holiness;
All idols spurn, for Christ was sacrificed.

Admonish idle folk; let work ensue;
Respect those over you now in the Lord,
And be at peace, and test the spirits true,
And help the weak to find where grace is stored.

The Lord will come from heaven with a shout,
And bring with Him the dead in Christ, who rise;
And after that, then we without a doubt,
Meet Christ up in the air—He glorifies.

May God Himself thus sanctify us whole,
And keep us blameless: body—spirit—soul.

II Thessalonians

53 Θεσσαλονικεις β΄

The <u>Second Book of Thessalonians</u>:
The persecution has increased the pain;
Thank God for your endurance, faithful hands,
Till Christ's return to praise—or hell's disdain.

The lawless man wreaks havoc on God's world,
But not forever—Christ redeems His own;
Recall Paul's teachings, and Christ's word unfurled;
Now His return is plain—as Paul makes known.

Now, some of you are leading idle lives,
Refusing proper work, the rich to leach;
But Paul, like Christ, in selfless service strives;
He'll cut and stich in making tents to preach,.

So may the Lord of peace now grant you peace,
And give you comfort, grace—all praise increase.

54 Τιμόθεον α´

First, Timothy, there is one God—a man,
One mediator, Jesus, our delight—
Divinity in flesh, God's perfect plan—
Was seen by angels, preached, then rose in light.

Set good example—never mind your youth;
Let modest women learn in quietness;
And love of money is no root of truth;
Providing not for kin is great transgress.

The overseers have a noble task;
They are above reproach, know how to teach,
Hospitable—you never have to ask—
And run their families well—in honor preach.

Now may the God eternal, God all wise,
Be He that man gives honor, glorifies.

55 Τιμόθεον β′

Paul's <u>second</u> word to <u>Timothy,</u> his son,
In Ephesus, he's called to teach, be bold,
And preach the word in truth till all are won,
And not to be ashamed of Gospel told.

God's Spirit guided men so what they wrote
Gives wisdom leading to a true belief
In Jesus the messiah—so please note,
It trains in righteousness for our relief.

So, if we died with Him, we'll live with Him;
If we endure, then with Him we will reign;
If we deny, then life with Him is dim,
But He'll be faithful and His name sustain.

The scriptures are God-breathed for training all;
I'm sanctified—my holy overhaul.

56 Τίτον

Paul's <u>Titus</u> stayed in Crete to mend church life,
Appoint some elders—disciplined—teach creed,
Hospitable, and husband of one wife,
Whose children are believers, without greed.

Impart sound doctrine—older men like me;
And women teach the younger ones in truth,
In self-control, good works, integrity,
Submissive to their husbands, love the youth.

God saves us not through our good works we own;
The Holy Spirit's mercy on us fell,
That we be justified by grace alone,
Heirs of eternal life, not dead in hell.

So overseers be above reproach,
And older women, younger ones should coach.

Philemon

57 Φιλήμονα

Philemon brother, please forgive your slave;
Receive him back now as a son of mine;
I will repay your dues, the grief he gave,
For you owe me the very life that's thine.

All Christian folk are equal partners true,
Partake in gifts of love and grace abound,
And bring all joy and comfort—hearts renew;
I've loved to have Onesimus around.

But now I ask to send him back to you,
And know that you will do what I request
To have him back a slave but brother too;
Prepare for me as well to be your guest.

All Jesus foll'wers share His love and place
As equal partners koinonia grace.

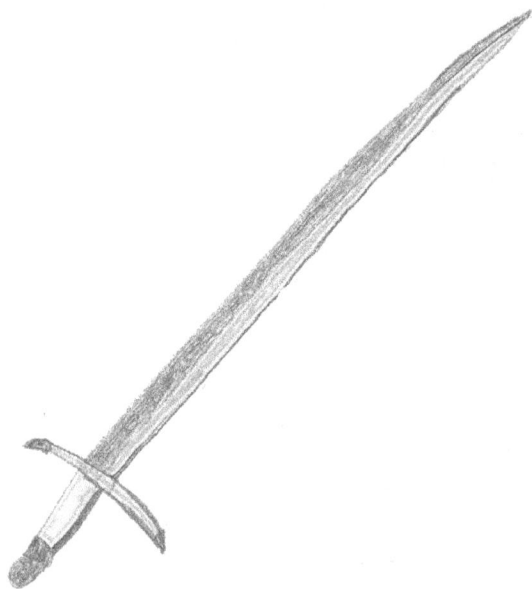

Hebrews

58 Ἑβραίους

Oh, <u>Hebrews</u>, Jesus is the same today,
Eternal and much superior thing
To angels, Moses, what priests do and say—
He's of Melchizedek, both priest and king.

Christ, our high priest who knows us from above,
Since He was tempted but without disgrace;
So let's think how to spur us on to love;
He promised to be with us in the race.

So meet together—welcome strangers, do,
For some are angels; some have faith that's strong,
Like Abel, Enoch, Noah, Rahab too,
And Abraham, his wife—the list is long.

I fix my eyes on Jesus—grace He poured,
The author of my faith, with two-edged sword.

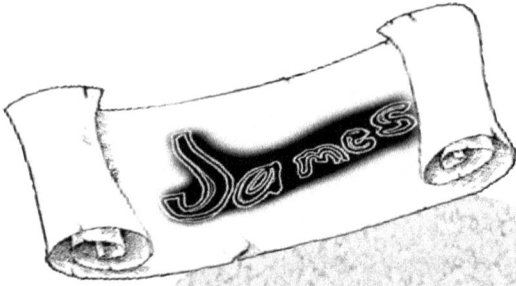

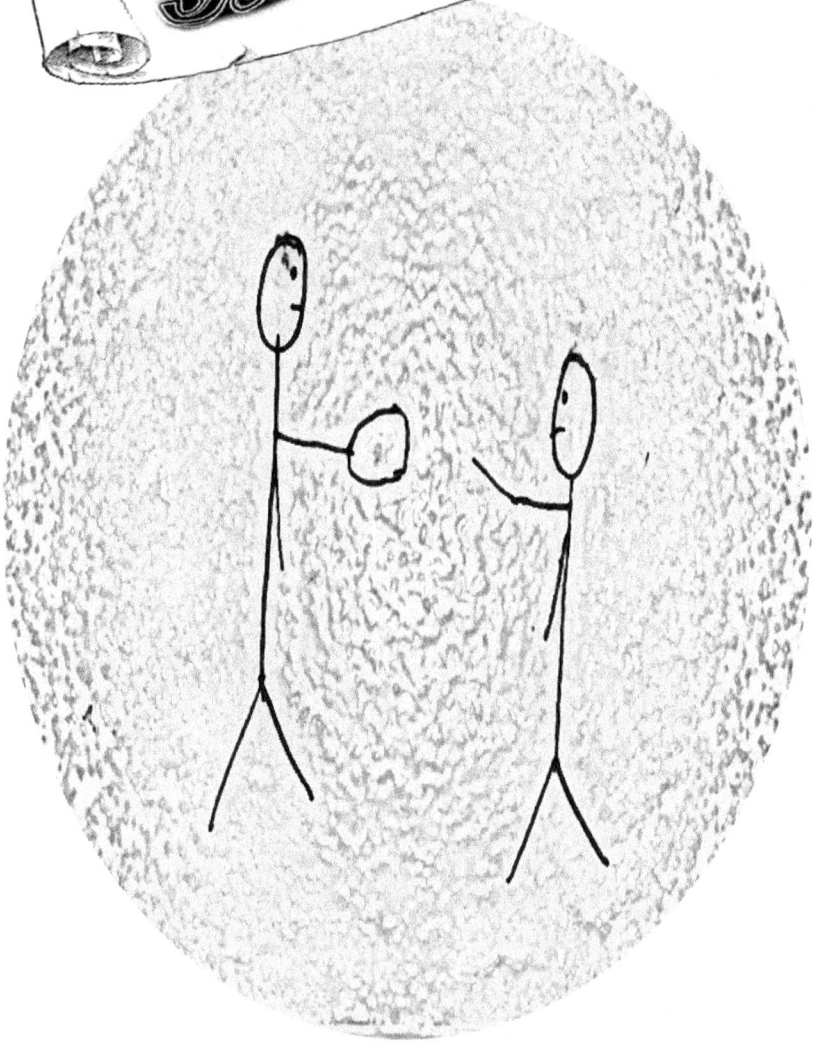

59 Ἰάκωβου

To worship Christ is preached by brother <u>James</u>,
To love impartially all men as one;
Since faith apart from works goes down in flames,
And wisdom from above is never done.

So do not love the world, to God submit;
Speak not against a neighbor, judging all;
Your wealth will rot with you, it's counterfeit;
Be patient now until the trumpet call.

So tell the truth and let your "yes" mean "yes."
The prayer of faith will heal and save and free;
Restore the brothers so that God may bless;
To love both God and neighbor—bend the knee.

You show me faith alone and boast of creeds,
But I will show my faith just by my deeds.

Peter

60 Πέτρου α´

First Peter tells of hope in suffering;
More gentiles now belong to Abraham,
A chosen people called from death to sing
The wonders of the mercy of the Lamb.

So in your heart prepare an answer true
For those who ask and doubt your hope is right,
That righteous Christ once suffered what we're due,
Was put to death and raised in Spirit might.

Now be alert and strong with sober minds,
The devil prowls and like a lion roars;
So honor wives as gentle, weaker kinds;
Unhindered grace in prayer will then be yours.

Yes, love each other—everybody wins,
For love will cover multitudes of sins.

61 Πέτρου β′

In <u>Peter's second letter</u> be aware
Participate in Christ's divine own self,
For this the Prophets spoke from God to share:
Escape the world's corrupting evil stealth.

But there were false, destructive prophets there;
"No final reckoning," they said, "We're free"—
Dumb animals, they'll die without God's care;
On Judgement Day real misery they'll see.

So why does God in patience never tire?
For Him one day is thousands unto men;
The earth and heavens pass in cleansing fire;
Behold new earth and heaven shout amen.

So add to knowledge, Godliness above;
To mutual affection, add your love.

1 John

62 Ἰωάννου α΄

First John—he writes on truth and life and love;
If we confess our sins God purifies,
Unrighteousness forgiven from above,
Abide in love, not darkness, death, and lies.

Since God is light, in Him no dark at all,
Come in the flesh for me, God's Child so fair,
To give His life that I might heed His call,
And love my brothers, fellowshipping there.

Do test the spirits, do they speak from God?
False prophets spread throughout a world of sin,
Denying Christ is king—and on they plod,
But God's dear children run and victory win.

Beloved, let us love each other well,
For God is love—and hate is straight from hell.

2 John

63 Ἰωάννου β′

John's second letter—to the mom elect,
And children of the truth in grace and peace,
Who walk in love and mercy circumspect,
From Christ, the Father's Son who'll never cease.

And this is love—to walk in His command—
From the beginning, this is not so new;
Take heed of what you've heard and firm you'll stand,
And sisters, brothers love each other true.

For false deceivers go throughout the land;
The antichrist blasts Christ come in the flesh,
And all who welcome him are bad and banned,
The wicked and the righteous never mesh.

Continue on in truth—is that so odd?
Abide in Christ or you'll not find your God.

64 Ἰωάννου γ′

The elder <u>John's third letter</u> to the church:
I pray for health of body and of soul;
Oh Gaius, I'll not leave you in the lurch;
You're walking in the truth; your joy's my goal.

Beloved, it's a faithful thing you do,
Supporting brothers going in God's name;
Though strangers, their reports of love are true;
Accepting naught from Gentiles for God's fame.

Please heed my writings, yet Diotrephes
Does not acknowledge our authority,
And speaks some wicked words, not just to tease,
And stops the brothers' welcome—even me.

Beloved, do not imitate the bad,
But follow good, God's blessings to be had.

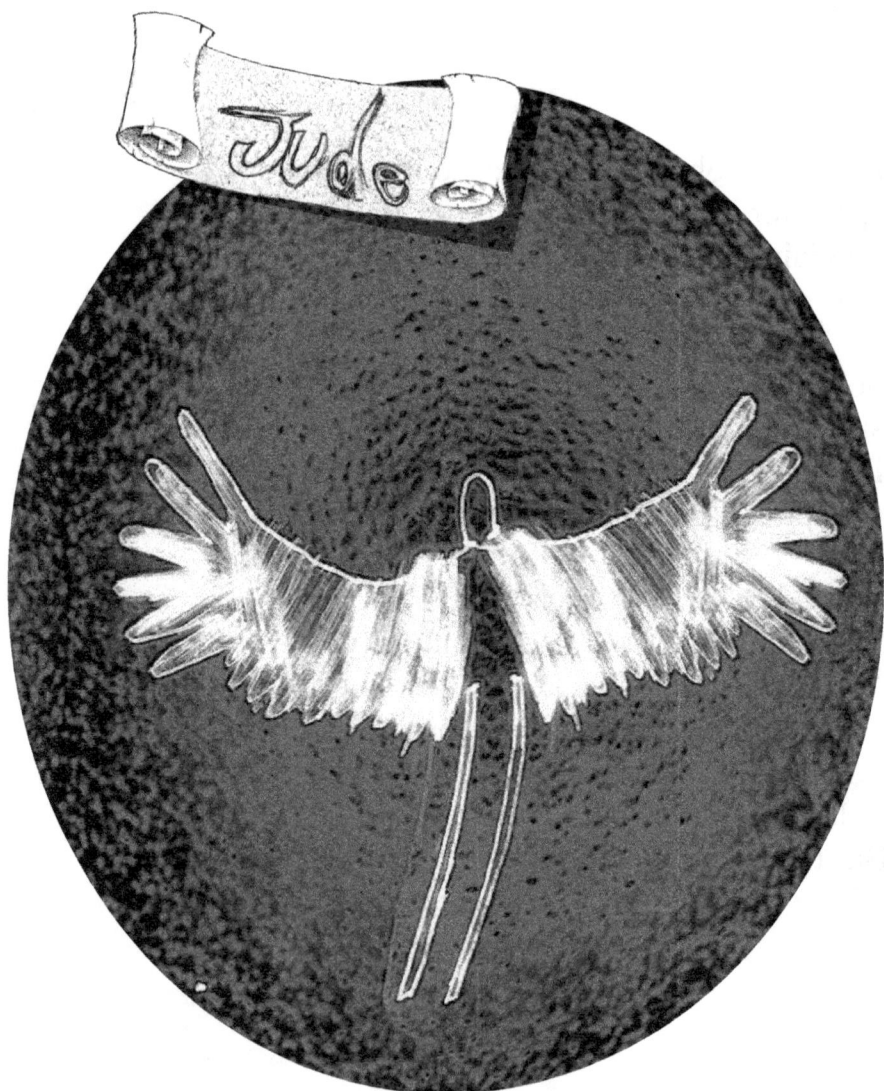

65 Ἰούδα

So Jesus' brother <u>Jude</u>, writes urgently,
For certain teachers creep into the church,
Pervert God's grace in sensuality,
And trash authority, Christ's name besmirch.

Rebellion judged by God's almighty hand:
The lustful angels come to wed young girls,
The faithless Jews before the Promised Land,
And Sodom's immorality unfurls.

The Lord rebukes, Archangel Michael said,
The devil—all those who corrupt and sin,
Like Balaam, Cain, the band that Korah led;
The end is near, so stay alert to win.

I praise the Lord who hears my grumbling,
Presents me blameless without stumbling.

66 Ἀποκάλυψις Ἰωάννου

The <u>Revelation</u> God displayed to John,
With seven churches, Christ the slain lamb deals;
He's Alpha and Omega—on and on,
And holy, holy worthy opens seals.

Of conquest, famine, war and death—how long?
So who is righteous on the Judgement Day?
From every tribe and tongue, a holy throng,
Christ's army, many martyred in the fray.

Then seven bowls poured Armageddon war,
Till Satan's thrown into the Lake of Fire;
A bright new heaven and new earth restore,
And every tear and pain and death retire.

Behold I stand outside the door and knock;
Please open so that we can sup and talk.

www.ingramcontent.com/pod-product-compliance
Lightning Source LLC
Chambersburg PA
CBHW070835100426
42813CB00003B/629